The Journey and the Grace

GARY A. WESTGARD
Gary A. Westgard

ISBN: 978-1-57579-354-2

Library of Congress Control Number: 2007925954

Cover photo by Gary Westgard
Southeast South Dakota

Printed in the United States of America

PINE HILL PRESS
4000 West 57th Street
Sioux Falls, SD 57106

to Vivian

I CORINTHIANS 12

We are like snowflakes,
but with tempers.

Table of Contents

"A poem is a record of a discovery, either the discovery of something in the world or within one's self, or perhaps the discovery of something through the juxtaposition of sounds and sense within the language."

- *Ted Kooser, United States Poet Laureate, 2004-2006*

Faith and Poems

Faith and poems are both about words. Faith is someone speaking or writing words and someone else hearing or reading those words, and believing them. Nothing can be proved, of course.

A poem is about someone choosing words, putting them together, one after the other, and someone else reading those words, and discovering they tell the truth. Nothing can be proved, of course.

The poems in this book are meager offerings: personal and simple. They are moments, little bits of time, records of discovery, some in memory, and some as I try to pay attention in this troubled, beautiful world which I love.

- *Gary A. Westgard*

The Journey and the Grace

Fathers, do not provoke your children,
lest they become discouraged.
- Colossians 3:21

We would visit relatives, and while
the parents sat around a table,
drinking coffee and talking, the
cousins would play until late into
the night. Then my sisters and I
would be piled into the back
seat of our car to begin the
journey home, knowing that
once we got into that back seat,
we had nothing else to attend to
or be concerned about until the
morning. When we fell asleep
in the back seat of the car, we
knew we would awaken in the
morning, in our beds. Dad would
carry each one of us into the house,
mom would pull back the covers,
and sometimes with only our
coats and shoes removed, we
would be tucked in for the night.
The truth of it was so comforting,
so kind, so reassuring and
wonderful, that sometimes
we would even pretend to
be asleep, just to enjoy
the journey and the grace.

Foolish Child

Foolish Child

They said I was a foolish child,
those of the same age as
my parents, though my parents
refused to agree, but only
expressed their fear,
as I too expressed my fear,
for the animal was twice as large
as me, and many times faster.
I thought he was held captive
 to his tree, as always,
but that evening, near dark, I
discovered otherwise. He had in the past
growled and jumped toward us children,
but we were safe, for he was connected
to a great large chain. We stood and
laughed at him, as we had before,
and then too late, saw he was
free to move about and free to run
after foolish children. Either the others
were faster or I looked more like a good
meal, for he came and closed his mouth
on my bottom. My scream brought rescue.
I was taken to a bedroom,
examined, bandaged and chastised.
Foolish child, they said. *He'll get
over it,* they said. Yes and no.

I Cannot Hear My Mother's Voice

I cannot hear my mother's voice,
nor see her in my head.
I look at old pictures,
it seems
to be someone else instead.
She who once held me in
her own body,
fed me her own food,
laid me in the crook of her arm,
pushed me off to school,
kept my secrets,
forgave my sins,
yet I cannot bring her home.
I do, for some odd reason,
remember her washing my hair.
I, standing on tiptoe in order to
lean my head forward under
the faucet of the laundry tub,
shivering in the cool morning air,
even as the warm water soaked
the back of my neck, got into my
ears and ran, a small stream,
over my head, washing me,
claiming me forever as her child.
Like a baptism.

Hoeing Thistles

My father asked me to take a hoe,
go out into the hilly field
and chop thistles.
I went out to the garage,
found the hoe,
walked out to the hilly field
with hoe in hand, and
found a comfortable place
in the tall grass,
just above the stream
that ran below the hill.
I made sure there were no
thistles in the grass
to scratch my soft skin,
then I lay down,
cap shielding my eyes,
hands folded behind my head,
the sun warm on my body,
the stream in view,
and stayed there until
mom called me in for supper.
A fine day for
hoeing thistles.

The Paper Mill

I worked at the paper mill
in the summer after high school
and between each year of college.
I worked at the paper mill
so I would never have to work
at the paper mill.
The men who worked full time
were good to me, glad I was
going to college, glad I would
not have to be there after four years,
glad because they wanted something
better for me, and glad because
I didn't know what the heck I was doing.
I remember thinking how good
it will be when I am done
working at the paper mill.
Well I have been done now
for more than 40 years
and I am still thinking
how glad I am to be done
working at the paper mill.

Lab Work

Down the stairs, two flights, basement room.
Morning paper divided between three chairs,
straight backs, built to last. Occupied by
strangers, who glance up when someone new
enters, then back to looking at their laps or
the television set hanging in the corner.
I assemble the paper, read until my name
is called by a smiling woman who leads me to
a separate place behind a wall. She taps my
skin just inside the elbow, telling me to make a
fist, as I turn aside and hum. She pushes
a wad of cotton over the tiny wound,
covers it with a bandage, saying, all done.
I thank her, slip on my jacket, walk
through the room of strangers toward the
stairway, thinking, *for this I am sent a bill.*

I Walk This Road

I walk this road,
past a place of animals: dogs barking
happily as soon as I am near, a horse
leaning against a fence, looking for
company (can't get a word in edgewise
for the dogs), buffalo, about 12 head,
see me coming and gather in committee
to welcome, dust flying as they run in
anticipation of friendship and a meal,
then stand rejected on the other side of
the fence. A car passes, throws a few rocks
in my direction, then hides behind a skirt
of dust. On the way home, a pasture,
unoccupied, littered with dark brown
mounds of dung, evidence of previous
residents - *droppings.* Something
blinks at me from the ditch, an empty
vodka bottle, and then all the way
home: beer bottles, pop cans, a
cardboard box, a part from a car,
a shelf for a cupboard - *droppings.*

The Tough Decisions an Old Retired Man Must Make Everyday

In the midst of an open field of brown,
the tall grass waiting patiently for the
spring collection of new bright colors,
there caught on something too far
away for me to see, is a white
sheet of paper waving at me,
waving all day, and I have
yet to decide if I should
wave back.

The Stories We Write

Riding the light rail in Minneapolis,
he gets on alone and sits across,
looking tired.
I will to silently greet him, to
welcome him to our community
of travelers, thereby bringing
a smile to his face,
but his eyes will not meet mine
and he sits in his own place.
I write his story then:
Up early this morning,
worked hard all day, now
back home to an empty house.
This sad, lonely man, whose
cell phone rings, and there comes
such a smile, as to make me laugh,
so while he talks and grins,
telling someone who loves him
he will be home soon,
I edit his story.

At the End of the Day

Where are your shoes?
The mother asks her barefoot child.
Where are your socks?
I don't know, she answers truthfully,
this one who has come in from
the joyful work of play,
I don't remember.

What is your name?
I ask, when I see a familiar face,
moving toward me in the room.
I begin working through the alphabet,
in the hope of stumbling upon my friend.
It never works. I must answer truthfully,
I don't remember.

What He's Doing

I suppose he knows what
he's doing, my neighbor,
who was out today,
late October, cold October,
fertilizing his lawn, the
grass cut short for
winter. I left my
grass three inches high.
Deep enough for mice
to hide in, a friend tells me.
But sturdy, I say, sturdy
until spring. I fertilized in
early October, warm October,
which seemed right. Still,
I tell my wife, he must
know what he's doing, my
neighbor. Like the President,
other elected leaders,
and the generals,
they must know what
they're doing, I tell myself.
Then I think, perhaps that
is what others say of me.
They say, he must know
what he's doing. But
most of the time,
I don't.

Toys

I am just passing through,
more days behind than ahead,
considering now how blessed.
I sit in this room surrounded by
memories from my childhood:
cap gun with holster and belt,
smiling piggy bank colored white and red,
copper colored horse with glued leg,
wooden airplane my father helped me build.
A child's toys.
An old man's memories.
Grace in porcelain, metal, and wood.
Dime store treasures that never
lose their ability to make me smile.
Love incarnate to this
always child.

One Fried Egg

One Fried Egg

- Albert Harold Westgard &
Beatrice Alvida Olson, 1940-1974

One fried egg,
a slice of toast, coffee.
My father's breakfast,
prepared by my mother
every work day morning,
in the kitchen of my
childhood. I sit,
still sleepy, on the
living room sofa, listening
to morning words, quiet
like secrets. She sits across as
he finishes his coffee, a kiss
at the door, off to work at
the mill. She clears
away the dishes, helps me
get ready for school. It
seemed then a place I should
not be, watching my parents
being husband and wife
in the early morning.

It was Better Back Then

It was better back then,
my grandfather used to say,
telling of neighbors
helping one another at harvest time,
families sitting at table on Saturday night,
drinking hot coffee, eating sandwiches
and angel food cake,
while the children played near.
Mostly he told
about people taking care of each other,
trusting one another.
He seldom mentioned
the summer work in the
fields, hot from morning
sun to dark, or the wood
stove always hungry in January,
the floor so cold it stung
your feet, or the outhouse 20
yards out back where an owl
guarded the summer,
demanding some form
of identification. Still
maybe he was right.

She's an Old Tree

- Gunder (Gunnar) Olson &
Selma Marie Haldorsen, 1915 - 1980

She's an old tree, branches bare,
some broken. The ground below
receiving life that used to be.
One day she got tired and tried to
lie down, came to rest against
the tree nearest. Since the
beginning, they have stood
next to one another, deeply rooted.
I stop now on this road to listen.
I hear him. *It's alright, I*
can hold you like this forever,
I won't let you fall.

It is my grandfather whispering to my
grandmother when she could no longer
care for herself, and he kept her in their
home until she died, never left her alone,
never let her fall.

I Saw My Father Cry Twice

The second time, I was standing next to him,
looking into the casket which held my mother.
Stone still, he whispered, *It should have been me.*
I should have gone first. He lived another
25 years, regretting far too many of them.
The first time, I was sitting on his lap in a
pickup truck, grandpa behind the wheel,
ready to begin the journey west,
leaving our North Dakota farm after
the barn got on fire, and he and my uncle
butchered the burned pigs. The farmhouse
he abandoned that day would remain standing,
an unburied corpse, for the rest of his life.
As grandpa started the pickup, I heard
a sound come out of my father, and in a
voice I did not know, he told me, so I turned
away, as I did 24 years later, when once again
he lost his life.

Hiding Places

There is a cave poked into
the three foot ridge of snow
along our neighbor's driveway,
big enough for a child to hide
away. My wife built such a
place in our basement, using
a card table and blankets,
where our grandson could
crawl inside. When I was
young, there was a place
behind the garage, for
pretending, being alone. When
I got older I went to the
library for much the same
purpose. My father would
stop at a tavern after work, a
couple miles from home.
Same thing.

Letter to My Father

My mother was dating another man,
when one evening you invited
her and her sister, Emma,
who was going with Jimmy, whom she
eventually married, to go for a ride in your car.
My mother and Emma accepted the
invitation. I can imagine how you
laughed together that evening.
Later my mother told the other man
she was seeing someone else.
On the day my mother had the stroke,
it was just the two of you again,
as you carried her in
the quiet of the house, where
no one heard your fear.
Not long after the funeral, you sold
the house where she still sat before
the mirror brushing her hair when
you would come home from the cemetery.
How ordinary the beginnings and the
endings of our world, the only world
we know, and how we hate to
leave, until we get to a place
alone, in a room, always looking
out, but not able to go there
anymore. Then you just want
to go to sleep and never wake up,
and one day that is exactly
what you did.

Such Quiet

The father lies in his last bed,
his oldest and youngest
child near.
They go to sleep
with sounds coming
out of him,
breath that wails,
curses in the night.
Startled awake by
silence,
the orphans wait for him,
watch for him,
not believing in such quiet,
in such a thing as
change.

Pictures on A Dresser

- for Beverly, Merna, Marie

I sit on a bed in Marie's house.
Before me is the way it used to be.
My three sisters, hair curled,
pink dresses, all smiling back at me.
I am there, my arm around one,
I, the oldest, the only son.
Not able to remember, I trust
the picture to be true. I see
our beginning and realize
again how we have come to
live in different places and
how life has worn us a bit,
how our struggles have
not been equal. We
do not now sit together
as we did then, but I am
thankful for that time, now distant,
seeing the world
from the safety of our
home, for we are not smiling
at the photographer.
Such a beginning is
not granted to all, so we were
blessed for sure. I smile
back at us now with affection,
remembering and trying to
remember, and regretting too,
that I did not pay more attention
to the girls in pink dresses.

It Will Not Be

On the day I learned my
father once rode two
horses at the same time,
Roman style, standing one
leg on each horse, I was
watching as he walked
over the grass, a crutch
under each arm, wearing
his work cap and jeans,
talking to a grandson,
the one who carries his
name along with the
dream that one day he
will farm the land my
father left almost a half
century ago, but it will
not be. He gave up his
pickup truck, when it
scared him to drive at
night, so he sat watching

as others drove too quickly
on the highway within
sight of his apartment,
wishing he could once
again grab his keys, jump
in and go, but it will not
be. I write of this man
who lived for 85 years,
and think back on all
we could have said to
one another, could have
told of dreams and
visited his youth, when
he rode two horses at
one time, Roman style,
standing one leg on each
horse, but it will not be.

In the Nursing Home

— *in memory Edith Weeks*

She never did get all her books read.
The pictures in the room tell stories that
no longer have meaning to anyone else.
All the stuff lined up on the bookshelf,
all the memories lined up in the head.
Trips long ago planned, now long ago past.
Parties over, decorations put away,
Christmas presents forgotten.
Names of friends that cannot
be brought to mind,
so dear at one time.
Relatives who look like their parents.
Children of children who don't know
what used to be and who used to be
important or famous. Nothing
in common. Nothing but
change promising fear, sadness.
Not hope, not anything good.
Waiting, always waiting.
In the room, at the table, in the hall.
Waiting for someone to take you to
the bathroom, waiting for dinner,
waiting for someone, a loved one,
anyone, to come and take you
home. Always waiting. Waiting
for sleep, endless sleep to take
you away from now. Waiting
impatiently for God to come.

Wedding Band

Wedding Band

- December 16, 1967

A lake in South Dakota
stole my wedding band, not
long after I got married to her,
but the lake could not know: I do
not need a wedding band to
keep me attached to her.

I Come Quietly

I come quietly
to our bed
in the morning.
She wants only to sleep.
I come and gently
rub her feet.
No words are spoken.
I wake her,
not wanting to wake her.
She peeks over the covers,
smiles.
She is twenty-one again, and
I am glad for another day
with her.

For Example

I know, for example,
she likes a pinch of salt
in her oatmeal, in the morning,
so when I make oatmeal for two
I put just a pinch of salt in the water.
I know, for example,
she doesn't like
to work the pump at the gas station,
so I go along and fill the tank,
and she always says thanks.
I know, for example,
she falls asleep
when we are watching TV
in the evening,
and she doesn't want me to wake her,
so I let her sleep until she is ready to be awake.
I know, for example,
she likes:
coffee in the morning,
asparagus,
a good steak,
cheese pizza with extra cheese,
that she puts more milk than necessary on her cereal,
she will leave the dishes until later,
she won't turn on any lights when we
come home in the evening, when it's dark,
so I stumble as I follow her
into our house,
again and again.

We are Much in Love

We are much in love,
marred now close to 40 years.
There is nothing she would
not do for me, and I would
do all for her. Yet,
must be something
has changed, something
has died, for last night,
when I followed her into bed, she
turned, then kindly whispered,
Please, you're on my side.

Forever

There are memories
only my wife and I share,
and when we are gone,
will disappear
forever,
like the love letters
we burned in the fireplace,
the words rising to heaven
for angels to read and
marvel at our love.

Always

I go to the kitchen cupboard to take
out a plate for lunch, set it down,
realize I have taken out two plates.
As natural as breathing, as lying down
next to her at night. She is at work
now, that's all, but I become afraid.
For these many years, always.
Always, I order two tickets.
Always, I reserve a table for two.
Always, I pour two glasses of wine.
Always, two names on the letter
at Christmas time.

Love Never Ends

I watch a video. My
grandson's first weeks of life.
I see my son, being tender with his son,
holding him gently, looking into his eyes.
I remember the tenderness of his
mother, how she held our son, how she
looked into his eyes. So even now, though
miles apart, she is teaching her
grandson to be kind and good,
gentle of heart.

Thoughts Before a Wedding

Of course, I'm old, what can I tell them?
That perhaps they will find disappointment,
wonder some morning, who is this
person? Ask, what if? My hope is
they may, by some grace, learn to
love one another, learn to be quiet and
kind with each other. I hold out for that
possibility. Falling in love is easy, an
accident. Loving another is of the
will, full of courage, taking more
humility than most people care to
muster. It may not be romantic,
but will do.

Pastor Standing Next to the Mother of the Bride

- for Linda Iverson

The candles have been lit.
The widowed grandmother
has been walked down the
aisle by her grandson, the groom,
who then guides the other grandparents
to their places up front.
The groom has two more trips,
one with his parents,
then the final walk with the mother of the bride.
I stand next to this woman who
has watched her oldest son
get married and move two states away,
who will soon sit helplessly as her
only daughter joins herself to this man
who is now coming back up the aisle,
to take her to a place she is not sure
she wants to go.
She turns to me and says,
I'm not going.

I understand.
I stood, in the afternoon, in the empty
bedroom of a daughter delivered to
college that same morning, remembering
another morning when she walked off to
kindergarten with the neighbor girl.
I turned my back on the airplane taking
our son over the ocean, and sat wiping
tears next his mother in the front row,
as he spoke promises to his young bride.
Every new place we enter,
every new walk we take, brings
with it a guarantee: it will not be
as it once was, not ever again.
So on this warm October afternoon,
when the mother of the bride
says, I'm not going, I turn to
her and say, *Good, if you're not
going, I'm not going either.* And then
we both go.

Hunting Elephants

Hunting Elephants

When visiting with my grandson,
who is two years old, he never
wonders aloud if he needs more
health insurance, or if he will
eventually find a job. He does
not concern himself with the
weather or the stock market.
He is not interested in what
he will wear tomorrow or if
I think his hair was cut a bit
too short the other day, or if
his shirt matches his pants.
He is not worried about the
President or the war in Iraq.
He does not question why he is
here, and what purpose his life
serves. He does not seem to
think about tomorrow or
even what we will have for
dinner tonight. He does ask
me to help him find an elephant,
apparently lost somewhere
in this room, which he plans
to put on his train. This
is the kind of problem I can
deal with and feel pretty good
about solving. He also appreciates
my efforts and rewards me with
a smile, which is not bad pay
for a guy my age with little
experience hunting elephants.

The Usher

- Joshua Allan Westgard
Nothing but good memories.

My six year old son sits in church,
with his sister and his mother,
this child who loves to play,
who would rather be any place other
then sitting in worship on such a beautiful day.
But a miracle happens, when at his feet
he sees one of God's more sturdy creatures,
a large box elder bug:
The Incredible Hulk of bugs.
In a moment of child-like brilliance,
Josh discovers the joy of giving as
he places his precious quarter on the back
of this tiny usher, then watches as it
slowly, faithfully, carries his offering
all the way up to the altar.

Sitting in Church

- Christin Linnae Westgard
Gratitude, always.

I reach for a pill bottle and
struggle to remove the cap.
My daughter, next to me,
quietly takes it from my hand,
quickly gives it back.
Opened.
In that moment,
I know.
No matter how
things come to be,
I have nothing to fear;
this child will always watch over me.
It is like finding faith.

Talking Heads

*- for Benjamin Magnus
and Samuel Finn*

Sixty-three years separate my grandson and I.
I lift him up before me now. Face to face,
we look into each other eyes, then
I gently bump my head against his.
He answers my bump with a bump of his own.
I bump.
He bumps.
He smiles.
I smile.
So it goes:
Bump.
Smile.
Bump.
Smile.
We are communicating.

My Two Year Old Grandson

My two year old grandson
is guiding trains over wooden tracks,
building bridges and tunnels, putting up
buildings, and planting trees on the carpet, when he
stops for no apparent reason, looks up at
me with a smile, and says,
Hi grandpa,
then goes back to his work.
Prayer is like this.

To Walk with My
Two Year Old Grandson

To walk with my two year old grandson
is to stop to shake a chain hanging from a pole,
is to kneel down before an upturned wagon to spin a wheel,
is to watch a bug crossing the sidewalk,
is to splash hands in a small fountain,
is to watch toy soldier ride up the escalator alone,
is to be in no hurry to get home.

Christmas Morning Leaving

My grandson plays with the string cord
hanging from the collar of my jacket,
as we wait for his parents to put things
in plastic baskets, which move under
a machine to tell the silent man looking
at the screen if these people are bringing
weapons on board, in order to take over
the plane later this morning, on the way to
Minneapolis. This one I hold is just past
two, his second Christmas with his
grandparents, and he laughs now
as I take the plastic knob on the
end of the string in my mouth,
take it out of his soft, small hand, and I
know that I have lived for 65 Christmas
Days, and calculate how many more I may
spend with him, and imagine if he will
remember me at all. For I know of my
grandfather only by my father's telling, how
he watched me play on the floor of the farm
house where my father slept as a child, but only
by his telling, no more, no memory, and now
I wonder if this child, who laughs with me,
will remember the one who bids him
goodbye on this Christmas morning.

O the Joy

Jessie, three years old, is
driving his race car down the track,
coming into the last turn,
traveling at over 100 miles per hour.
His mother, sitting in a folding chair
in front of the garage, calls out,
Jessie, come home now,
don't leave the sidewalk.
Jessie turns in the saddle,
gives his gallant black
steed a gentle nudge and
gallops for home,
peddling slowly.

Mother and Son

- for Jacob and his mom

They stop at a pool of water left by the rain.
She sits on the sidewalk, legs crossed under,
places small pebbles before him. He squats,
his bottom almost touching the ground,
takes a stone in his full tiny fist, raises
his arm high over his head and throws
almost straight down, laughing as the water
splashes softly. Bringing his arms to his side,
holding his body in a joyous hug, he stamps
his feet in a little dance. They repeat this joy
over and again. Soon he will go off to
school, find other games to play,
other friends to play with. But on this
day, in this time, they are here, mother
and son, both looking for something and
both finding it.

September Comes

A sweet child
is coming. She runs and
puts a hug around my legs, leans her upper body
back to show off her new earrings, smiling up at me,
while her sister and the babysitter wait patiently.
After telling me about her trip to the mall,
she lets go of my legs, walking backwards to
get in as much talk as possible. She waves,
then turns and falls in with her sister.
I watch as she skips into the sun,
then become afraid.
I think of her summer ending,
going off to places where new
words are heard from
the mouths of God's children,
and the comfort of a mother's lap must wait
until the yellow bus brings her home.
Will she soon hide inside,
like my friend from long ago, who
with sad eyes, said, *When*
people tell you, you are an Indian, in such a way
to make you feel ashamed of who you are, worthless,
a lie told over and again, finally it becomes the
only truth that matters.
So said my friend, looking down.
A sweet man.

Cherry Coke

Cherry Coke

I sit in my chair, almost an old man,
to drink a cherry coke, and

with the first sip travel back
to high school, to

Jim and John, twin brothers,
and the YMCA

lunch counter, where
we laughed,

while drinking
cherry cokes.

Now I am back there
once again. So

here's to you my young
friends. You did not

know, nor did I, that
when we said

good bye that spring
afternoon, outside

the Y, it would
have to do

for a lifetime.

Friendship

*- for Tom and Jo, Darwin and
Kathy, Sam and Mary*

We are landscaping the yard.
Friends come to help. It is
only goodness on their part, for
we do not help with
their yards, or anything else,
for that matter. We merely
say, *Thank you,*
thank you very much.
Which seems quite pitiful,
considering all they do for us.
But it's what we give: words and
more words, and our
friendship, of course. Which,
apparently, is not all that great.

Shoveling Snow

- for Wade Brenden

I am out on my driveway
shoveling off the night snow,
retired now, so have no place to go,
no reason to be in a hurry,
but for the fact I will be glad
to be done shoveling snow.
Wade drives by in his pickup truck,
stops,
grabs a shovel from the back
and with a smile
begins to work from the other
side of the driveway.
We talk and shovel for
10 minutes, and
I have reason to
appreciate snow.

Beast of Burden

- for Joy Nelson

The small woman knells,
speaking into the just weaned donkey,
rubbing the head, behind the ears,
down the neck. Were it possible,
she would lift this frightened
creature into her arms and
rock her gently.
The woman knows she will come to this barn
at least twice in the night, a night with
no mother to rest up against, to comfort
this one with delicate feet, whose
ancestors were set apart to carry
on their backs the burdens placed
upon them, who has come to this ranch,
set apart to bear this woman's burdens
with her eyes.

In the Library

She is five, maybe six,
no older, trying to
get her mother's attention.
But mom is talking to
a friend, standing close,
as women will do, face to face,
looking into each other's eyes,
listening and talking and
listening, taking turns,
but hardly stopping to
wait between words,
glad to be in the presence
of one another.
So the daughter
must wait, perhaps until
she is able to look into her
mother's eyes, face to face.

Rhetorical Questions

The girl is about four,
the mother thirty years older.
They are walking in a hurry,
walking in an airport.
The daughter shouts,
I have to go to the bathroom.
The mother asks,
Who has to go to the bathroom?
The daughter answers,
I do.
The mother asks,
Now?
I don't hear the child's response.

The Evening News

Is this the world we live in,
where a 19 year old mother
puts her new born child
into a garbage can?
She who looks like your
average babysitter,
the shy, cute girl in the
class picture, second row.
Three years ago she was going to
high school football games and
giggling in the hall.
Now she looks at the camera,
tearless, dressed in orange.
How can one explain such a thing?
What reason can we give
for tossing babies in with the trash
on Friday morning, early, before
the truck goes by and misses us
this week?

Thanksgiving Day

Our daughter calls, tells
us her friend has been in
a car accident. The sister, who was driving,
broke both legs, their mother
was killed, the friend has a broken
neck. Maybe the sister fell asleep, our
daughter doesn't know. My wife and I are at home,
watching the Vikings win. Our
daughter is in North Carolina, visiting her
brother, playing with her nephew, helping
her sister-in-law with the new baby. Her
friend is in an Omaha hospital on this day
when people gather to give thanks for the
blessing of family.

How to Help Yourself
Not Feel Old

For one thing, don't look at photographs
taken recently; get out pictures from a few
years ago. Don't catch a glimpse of yourself
in a mirror or window as you walk down the street.
Spend time with younger people, especially those
with kids in school. Get up early in the morning,
tell everyone you enjoy it, and mean it.
Don't join AARP. Don't watch the Price is Right.
When a sales person assumes you get the senior
discount, get upset, even lie. Be married to a
younger woman from the beginning, but don't
marry a younger woman now, you will only
embarrass yourself and your kids. Don't
go to the local senior center, and don't
ever play bingo. Don't go south for the winter;
stay where you are, tough it out. Die young.

Stories in the Airport

Those are stories walking by,
as I sit in the Baltimore Airport
waiting to fly to Minneapolis.
Stories in a hurry to
get to a plane, pick up
luggage, say good-by
to family.
Stories deserving to be heard. But
I catch only a sentence or two,
as they move quickly by,
so I don't know the tale
from beginning
to end, and I wonder
what chapter this is
for me and for them.

The Auction

We crowd around the hay wagon,
like hungry puppies, while two
men stand looking down upon us,
one pointing a finger at an old friend,
the other doing a sound check on the
portable microphone, both trying
their best not to step on the boxes,
full of dishes, old tools, mason jars,
which will be sold first, then moving
on to the larger items, four matching
chairs, a sewing machine that hasn't
been used for a generation, an iron
bed, a 100 year old stone crock jar, no
cracks or chips, a kitchen cupboard
with the original light stain turned
dark by the passing of time, and
finally the John Deere tractor, pulled
in from the trees at the back of the
house, which will soon be hauled
away to be set in someone's barn or
garage, shined and tuned, ready for
the next small town parade, driven
by the new owner's grandson, and
we do not notice that the owners of
the boxes and chairs and the green
tractor are not among us, but inside

the house, afraid of revealing the
sadness they know this day, for the
neighbors gathered here only know
that the old couple will move into
an apartment in town, with no road
to clear in the winter, no yard to tend
to, no chores to finish before bedtime,
and they are glad for them and do not,
cannot, understand the great grief they
feel this day as their lives are held up
before neighbors and strangers and sold
to the highest bidder, that what is being
sold today is not merely tools and furniture
and dishes, but fifty years of living, piled
unto a hay wagon, carried out to the front
yard, and while anxious buyers count
plates and cups, lift up a flower vase
to find a name, pull out a drawer to see
how it was cut, nobody says a prayer
for the two people inside the old house,
now walking through each room, their
footsteps echoing in the empty space,
now stopping to embrace.

A Life Forgotten

- for Carl and Florence Stahl

Carl seldom recognized his own
children, but always knew his
wife. She came in the afternoon,
sat next to him on the side of
his bed to look at old photos, or
at a table in the dining room
to drink coffee. He still enjoyed
a cup of hot coffee and he could
still remember sadness when she
left, not understanding why she
would not take him home, but
she knew when she was out the
door, he would have already
forgotten she had been there.
The deep things were still in
him, like the Lord's Prayer,
which he could pray, word
for word, as he kept with me.

When his pastor came to visit,
though we had not known
each other before, he would
greet me like an old friend,
maybe pretending like the rest
of us pretend, that everything is fine.
Thank you, I'm fine, and you?
The last time we sat in the midst
of his community, I put my hand
on his head and blessed him, and
a woman near, reached out her
right hand, almost touching my
face, she pleaded, *Give me that,*
give me some of that.
Yearning to be blessed, to have
God place a hand on our heads
to tell us we are not forgotten,
even when we no longer are able
to remember who we are and
what we have done with our lives.

The Afternoon Paper

- for Oliver and Junice Wolden

They sit in the lobby, she on the couch,
he in his wheelchair, reading
the afternoon paper, as they did
before. Soon she will leave,
go to their car and drive home, as
he is pushed to the elevator,
which will take him to the second floor
dining room, to be seated at table with three
others, all with bibs in place, not hearing
one another, while kind women help.
He says he is satisfied living here.
He remembers, as his wife
left, she leaned down and kissed
his cheek and said *I love you*. After fifty years, it
is what they have.

A Tractor is Resting

A Tractor is Resting

A tractor is resting in some tall grass,
inside a grove of trees, facing away
from corn recently planted. It appears,
from a distance, it could be started and
driven, put back to work, but it's been
here now for three summers, so chances
are it will sit in these trees, season after
season, facing away from the life that
grows near, like an old man only
remembering.

Small Town

- for Carl and Mildred Christensen

While playing golf with friends, Mildred announced
She had a roast cooking at home, which was done
When we reached the fifth hole where we left
Our bags when we told the club manager
We would be back in two hours.
He said,
Fine.

Winter Frost

Some trees out back, naked since fall,
decided it is simply too cold, that's all.
So before I got up this morning, they
put on a little something in white:
Gowns that sparkle in morning's light.
But, I know, and they mean no harm,
they will undress again. Too warm.

The First Snow of the Season

The first snow of the season puts an end to
the reckless days of whistling, dreaming.
Back to small measured steps, the foot barely
lifted, the eyes watching the ground as if
searching for treasure. We learn to drive
again, both hands gripping the wheel,
alert, afraid of the brake, radio turned off,
praying to God while cursing the driver
following too close, as we slowly guide our
lethal weapons down the street.

Once safe inside, we talk, laugh nervously, at
not being able to stop at will, of going in circles
like Shriners in a parade. Yet proud, as if
winter was planned, our idea, making fun
of those who escape before November,
running like fugitives to Florida, frightened
conservatives, so careful. Winter was made
for liberals, open to new possibilities, looking
for someone to dig out of a snow drift, setting
up a committee to study the matter.

A Nuisance Snow

It's a nuisance snow.
The radio promised a real snow,
that does it's generous deed.
The kind of snow that gives good reason
to call in and say,
I can't make it today.
The kind of snow
that gives hope to children
in the early morning,
with the radio
tuned in to the local news,
waiting for the list
of cancellations,
silent prayers going up to God
as they go about
getting ready,
just in case.
The kind of snow
that can be used in construction
of primitive weapons,
to be turned against unsuspecting relatives.
But no.

This is a nuisance snow.
It provides no reward.
Stuck hard where civilization treads,
it only turns into something mean
and slippery, that it might do its nasty deed
and send someone to the hospital.
This is the troublemaker,
with no redeeming value.
If it were a real snow,
a good neighbor would come to my house
to show off his new snowblower.
But no.
My broom doesn't pick it up.
The shovel is over qualified.
Even the snowmobiles are silent.
I try to ignore it.
Slight, weak, a lame excuse.
But here it is,
as if it were the real thing.
A pretender and a nuisance,
refusing to be ignored.

Winter's Gift

- *for Jaime and her boys*

It's dark at five o'clock and I get stuck in
the driveway, backing quickly,
thinking I don't have to shovel
if I drive fast, but I am as wrong as
I was last winter. The girl next door,
out with her two children, playing
in the snow, laughing at the snow,
laughing still as she helps me push
until the back tires catch pavement,
then gathers one little one up in her
arms and heads home, calling the
other to *come now.* A few minutes
later, driving with my wife, we see
three young men studying a car
which is almost off the street. We
stop, get out, joke about stuck cars
and missed classes as we push to no
avail whatsoever, yet *thanks for stopping
and have a nice day.* Thus is shared
poverty, the stuck helping the stuck,
for something happens when snow
comes, full of violence, when nature
gets mean, we become nicer.
Sometimes.
Maybe.

South Dakota Rural

The dust of the street follows us into the
antique shop, then settles down to stay.
A screen door, at the back, claps twice
to announce her moving out of the
shadows into the light coming through the
front window and open door. Hands
pushing down her hair, smoothing
her skirt, she talks as she enters.
The wind is blowing so hard the clothes
dry as soon as I hang them on the line.
We study tables covered with
pink dishes, worn tools, salt and
pepper shakers, old Fisher Price
toys, then ask, *How is business?*
She confesses, *This is a dull town, no one*
wants to come here anymore and my sign
out on the main road is gone. It was
too heavy for even the wind to blow down,
so it's hanging in some stranger's house.
I don't understand people anymore.
It's not safe for a child to walk home
from school alone. She follows us
out to the empty street. *Windy,* she says,
the wind always blows in South Dakota.
Windy, windy, windy, but who would want
to live anywhere else?

Two Signs

Above the bookstore:
Finding God's Will. Details Inside.
Parking lot is empty.

Above the tavern:
Free Beer Tomorrow.
Place is packed.

Country Road

The only mailbox
on this mile of gravel
road, mouth open,
tongue hanging out,
looking like it hasn't
been fed in years,
and it doesn't look
promising.

I Shall Miss Bananas

I Shall Miss Bananas

God saw everything God had made,
and behold, it was very good.
- Genesis 1:31

I shall miss bananas
in the morning,
soaking in milk, covered with sugar,
sweet.
I am much in love
with this world.

No Music Played

No John Williams score played
as he went under for the third
time and stayed. There was no
one around to hear the sound
of his cries, and no music played.
If a portion of some beautiful
concerto could be heard when
the spouse announces this word:
I have found another, will
be moving out today.
If we could hear the soft notes
of a flute as the doctor begins,
I have some bad news.
A flute would help or a
violin.
But the only sound is
the sound of a practiced voice
saying: *She is at peace.* Or
the soft voice of a
funeral director, while
filling out the standard
forms, or the distant voice
of family trying to find
words they don't
wish to speak.
In life there is no
background music.
It's mostly quiet,
except for the
crying.

Musical Comedy

I watch this movie, a
musical comedy, in

Technicolor, filled with
beautiful people:

men, lean,
strong,

women with perfect
hair, long legs,

eyes full of mischief.
Everyone is

smiling, perfect
teeth. In

unison tap, tap, tap
dancing. Singing

songs of love, and
happy endings.

Then I realize,
everyone

in the movie
is dead.

What Are We to Do

Her husband would die
today. The doctor told her
in the early morning,
as we sat together in the
hospital waiting room.
We talked of his death.
She cried, made plans,
wrote down phone numbers
of people she would call.
I understand, she said,
I'll be alright.
In the late afternoon
the doctor came.
Your husband is dead.
She almost fell from her chair.
She kept saying, *It can't be true,*
he can't be dead. What am I to do?
What am I to do? She couldn't
find the phone numbers.

Last Talk With Jim

- in memory Jim Johnson

When we first met,
he talked about
hauling a truck load of
rocks to Minneapolis,
getting a better price for field
stone than for corn. Made him
angry so he didn't do it again.
Now he sits on the edge of
a hospital bed, both of us pretending
a hospital bed in the living
room is a common thing, while
he tells of his daughter,
who will run in the Boston
Marathon. We say goodbye
as if we will talk again,
for death still surprises.

Goodbye

- in memory Paul Larson

Goodbye my friend. It is
too soon to say goodbye.
You have fields to walk,
babies to hold. I know
you must leave, but I want
you to stay. It seems we
met only yesterday. You
are a good man. Your faith
as plain as a South Dakota
season, no doubt about its
meaning. Your leaving
makes my eyes water, my
soul ache. I must believe
God is not done, and three
days after Good Friday
there will be an Easter
morning, but it is not easy to
believe. I think I am most
like Thomas.

Old Enough

- for Roger and Lori Rust

Scottie was five years old.
Scottie was old enough to play catch,
run fast, tell a joke,
which made him laugh.
Scottie was old enough to say the ABC's,
count 1, 2, 3.
He was old enough to tie his own shoes
and brush his teeth when told.
Scottie was old enough to help mom
with the dishes and
ride next to his dad on the tractor,
which he loved.
Scottie was five years old.
Scottie was old enough to fall.
Scottie was old enough to die,
which he did.
It doesn't make any damn sense at all.
I'll never be old enough.

Picture

of a child
on a table
by the couch
a boy of five
old picture
old house
occupied by
old people
who is this child?
our son they say
our son who said
his stomach hurt
our son taken
to the doctor
our son who died
fifty year ago
our son who will
always be five

Blackjack Gum

As I get out of the car, the cold air
ushers my hands into jacket pockets,
where I feel the ragged paper and
pull out the blue and black pack
of Blackjack Chewing Gum,
purchased over a year ago, on
the day we had lunch, and the two
wives whispered about the cancer
over soup and sandwiches, while
Carl was in the bathroom, and I
was buying this gum from my
childhood, and here I am still
trying to keep what is past,
as I bring this package to my
face, smelling memories, a
fine day of generous laughter
and kind conversation when
Carl ordered only soup.

A Year After the Death of a Child

- in memory Devon Arthur Curtin

On the 365th day, I broke, she said.
I'm having a hard time of it, she said.
My family tries to help, but I hurt them, she said.
I wish it could have been me, she said.

Goodbye to My World

She knew she would die soon,
even without the doctor's words.
She knew it in her bones. It
was not death she feared, but
sleep. She said, *I do not*
want to die in my sleep.
I want to know when I leave.
I want to say, I will miss you, and
hear you say, you will miss me. I want to
know when I leave. I want
to say goodbye to my
world.

This Truth

- in memory Frank Slagle

For a moment, at the
intake of a breath,
he is still with us. Then
I breath out and know
again this truth:
What she said
when I came to see him
in the hospital, when I met
her in the hall, *he left us,*
eyes beginning to fill.
He left us, she whispered,
as she wrapped her arms
around my neck and sobbed,
he left us. Someone is always
leaving, until we leave.

Such Trust

Such Trust

- for Jennifer Brenden, mother

Would you like to hold her,
the mother asked. How
gracious, such trust,
to bless me this way,
her child just born,
placed in my arms.
Like God trusting us.
Would you like to hold him,
hold my son, gently, gently.
Hold one another,
gently, gently.

Practice

If only we could practce
for what comes later.
Practice being old.
Practice being alone.
Practice being orphans
and widows and divorced.
But we are called to go
out there, with no idea
how to do it, how to play
the game, how to survive.
No idea how bumped
and bruised we will get
out there on that field that
looks alien, so strange,
large and dangerous.
We thought we would
never have to suit up,
ever.

The Time it Takes

Lincoln's Gettysburg Address is 272
words long. It took two minutes to
deliver. When the president sat
down, someone asked, is that all?

As I get into my car, put the key
in the ignition, I notice a friend I have
not seen for almost a year, getting
out of her car. She walks by and we
look at each other through the front
windshield of my car, and there
is a moment, a slight hesitation
when we both think to come to
one another, maybe talk for a
time, but we don't. We wave and
smile, and she continues to walk,
as I start the car and back away.

Traveling from Sioux Falls to
Watertown, I consider a stop in
Brookings, to fill the car with gas,
maybe have a bite to eat, but decide to
save a couple minutes, get home early.
North of Brookings, a large deer
comes out of a ditch and looks me
in the eye, just before I slam into
him going 75 miles per hour.

The Magi

Where is he who has been born king?
We have come to worship him.
- Matthew 2:2

Christmas.
Late in the morning,
the phone rang.
A woman who lived down the street,
alone, was found dead in her kitchen,
found by a friend who called. I walked
through the deep snow, the air cold
and still, people safe in their homes.
I opened the back door.
There she lay on the floor
covered by the afghan
from her sofa, hair uncombed,
the smell of fresh coffee cooking,
an empty cup on the cupboard,
the house so quiet you could hear it.
The caller friend went out to shovel
snow off the front steps for the police
and ambulance. I looked out the window.
Another neighbor was clearing the driveway.
Together we would wait for family to come.
We didn't much talk for we were in the
presence of mystery, privileged to be summoned.

John the Baptist and Simon Peter

John answered, ". . . he who is mightier than
I is coming, the thong of whose sandals
I am not worthy to untie;"
- Luke 3:16

John
narrowed his life to one task:
Master of ceremonies,
introducing the main
speaker.

Satisfied with that.

Not worthy to carry the man's shoes,
was his best boast.

Not a way
to get elected
or be remembered.

Jesus said to Simon, "Do not be afraid;
from now on you will be catching men."
- Luke 5:10

Simon
only wanted to spend his life
fishing.

Which is what he did.

Matthew

*Jesus saw a man called Matthew
sitting at the tax office; and he
said to him, "Follow me."*
- Matthew 9:9

In my imagination, I
see Matthew as one of the
kids who always got picked
last. You remember, when
you were a kid with a bunch
of other kids, and someone said,
lets play, lets choose sides, and
the two most popular kids
always get to be the captains,
and they begin to choose other
kids to be on their team, until
everyone is chosen, except you.
Then one of the captains says,
you get him. That is how
I see Matthew. The kid who
always got left to the end of
the choosing, until one day
when he was at work,
collecting taxes.

Five Loaves and Two Fish

*Jesus said, "They need not go away
you give them something to eat."
- Matthew 14:16*

We have nothing here,
the disciples say, we have
five loaves and two fish.

We have something here,
Jesus says, we have
five loaves and two fish.

We cannot help them,
the disciples say, with
five loaves and two fish.

We can begin,
Jesus says, with
five loaves and two fish.

The world needs more,
the disciples say, than
five loaves and two fish.

Much of the world has less,
Jesus says, than
five loaves and two fish.

Send them away,
the disciples say, we have
five loaves and two fish.

They need not go away,
Jesus says, we have
five loaves and two fish.

Pentecost

- for Sam Vinella

They are two children at play,
though only one
is a child.
She is past 50
and he is 12.
They stand close,
looking to the sky,
arms outstretched.
The string that
flows from their hands
to the clouds,
as fine and fragile
as faith.
The wind
blowing
like the Holy Ghost,
unpredictable,
at times causing chaos,
as plan and hope is
crashed to the ground,
at times bringing laughter,
as they link their lives to heaven
and to one another.
Their joy as much
about friendship
as success. For
if they do not fly
it will still be a
very good afternoon.

Still Able

The car in front of us
stops in the middle
of the road. We sigh
loudly, berate the
driver, pass by,
look in the window,
see an old man
bewildered,
curse ourselves for
being so fortunate as
to be still able
to say terrible things
about people in
trouble.

Faith, Hope and Love

So faith, hope, love abide,
these three; but the greatest of these is love.
- I Corinthians 13:13

Faith
is fine as it is.
Do not confuse it with
another thing.
Let it be what it is.
A gift,
humble.
It must always love.
Such is its strength.
And fragile.
Doubt is likely around the corner.
Tomorrow maybe.

Hope
is a cat,
comes to sit on your lap
when you least expect her.
Turns twice around
before she lies down
to bring her comfort.
Let her stay.
She may not.

Love
is best, of the will,
more than the heart.
Better purpose,
than passion.
Better quiet,
than loud.
Better humble,
than proud.

Another Deadly Sin

The Bible warns of the following:
immorality,
impurity,
licentiousness,
idolatry,
sorcery,
enmity,
strife,
jealousy,
anger,
selfishness,
dissension,
party spirit,
envy,
drunkenness,
carousing,
and the like,
and mostly we know
such things are not right.
I, in my advanced years,
would like to add another,
oft exhibited, but
not as glamorous as others,
nor as much fun.

This sin is practiced by
some of religious fervor,
selling books and miracles on TV,
encouraging us to plant a seed,
to prove how much we believe,
and by those who aim to entertain
by yelling at any who disagree,
making fun, taking away
a person's dignity,
and, yes, by some elected to
high office, who claim
a much clearer view,
who have the responsibility
to help the rest of us through,
but who, I am afraid, are,
like the forenamed others,
captured by this sin
difficult for sinners to see:
the arrogant sin of
stupidity.

August 29, 2006

Today, in South Dakota,
we plan to kill a man,
the state, all of us, so
students in school
have the opportunity
for discussion, and over
lunch, between bites,
old men can debate
gas prices and lethal
injection, and a woman
questioned at the mall
says she wants to
be there to watch, but
a high school student
has homecoming
to plan, so hasn't
thought much about
this man who will die,

who did a terrible
thing, who killed
another human being,
and today we plan to show
this man how wrong
it is to kill another
human being, by
killing a human
being. Today, in
South Dakota the
shepherd will leave
the ninety-nine in the
wilderness, go off
after the one which
is lost, and when he
has found it, he will
lay it on his shoulder
and cut its throat.

The Sound of Easter

The Sound of Easter

- Mark 16:1-8

The sound of Easter
is the sound of running feet,
naked, small, calloused and brown,
fleeing the unknown,
women wordless
in their terror.

Christmas

Pain.
A cry.
Tears.
A slippery weight of flesh
and God appears.
Strange this night.

Most of What Counts

Most of what counts
cannot be seen.
Like the air.
Hopelessness, for example.
Maybe in the eyes.
Faith is not seen,
yet it can turn us into saints
or murderers.
We stand over the grave
of someone we love,
dare tell the world
he or she is doing quite well,
only not here with us today.
All the while counting on
something we do not see.

Only Darkness

Ahead of me on this gravel road,
a lone man is pulling a ladder
off a truck.
Nothing here to climb.
No building.
No tree.
Near the truck a cover for a sewer.
Down, he says, I'm going down.
I look into the hole.
Only darkness there.
He goes into the darkness.
You never know what you may find,
he says, with a smile on his face,
understanding life better than most.

The Lord's Supper

Small morsel of
bread, sip of wine,
and words: *eat,*
my body, drink,
my blood. We come,
bent over,
hands open,
reeking of wasted lives
or full of righteousness,
quiet for a time,
holding God in our
hands, in our mouths,
swallowing.

Preacher

60 people here. Were it a
cathedral with a thousand
souls sitting at attention,
he would do no more. Up
late, worried through the
text, admitting he does
not always understand,
nor believe, so is with us
in the struggle. His words
doing battle with other
words heard each day,
as hard to believe as
the words this old
preacher speaks this
morning, which hold
out the possibility
of hope.

Please Preacher

Please preacher,
don't tell me what to do.
Don't tell me what not to do.
Don't tell me if I do certain things
I will be successful, or
if I believe, I will be safe, or
if I really believe,
I will be prosperous.
Use words to show me
the world in which I live.
Tell me who I am
by telling me stories.
Let me stumble upon
myself in your words.
Tell me about God,
the great and
terrible God who seems not to hear, who
seems far away most of the time.
Hold out the possibility that
such a God cares about this world,
faith or no faith.

Tell me about Jesus.
Tell me what he did and
what he said,
how he lived,
how he died.
Dare tell the strange, wonderful
story of Easter.
Tell me I am a sinner,
but don't tell me, I'll get over it.
Tell me how much
God loves sinners.
Tell me about the cross and
what it means,
where it is,
why it is.
Leave me to decide
what to do with
your words.
Let me know
you struggle with faith
as much as I.

The Holy Man

The holy man is coming out of his house
on Monday morning, hooked to his dog,
walking over the grass, stopping
as the dog squats.
Yesterday the holy man stood in
a holy place, held in his hands
the bread and wine of the
Holy Sacrament. Today he is out
in the world cleaning up shit.
It is what holy men do.

Worship at the Monastery

- to the Sisters at Mother of God

We come together, about twenty of us,
in the almost dark, candles bright
at the front, singing short sentences
in Latin, listening to old words read,
throwing requests in the air in the
hope that God will catch a few. There
is something to be said for believing
against all odds. It is easy to believe
the sun will rise tomorrow, flowers
and trees will bloom in the spring, or
even gas prices will eventually go down,
but to believe the dead will be raised or
we will learn forgiveness, now that is
faith. Saints have it, and children,
and there are saints in this room for
sure. The rest of us are here practicing
to be children once again.

The Importance of Death

It is late, the meeting over, others
have left for home, but I want to
stay awhile, on this quiet, cloudless
night, here in the country, sit on
the front steps of this old church,
look across to the cemetery, a few
steps away. Old stones sunk in
the ground. Newer stones where
I have stood. You can't enter this
church without seeing the graves
of all who have come before and
those we had come to love.
Sacred ground. A sign.
Death is not off in some far country.
Helps a preacher tell the truth, helps
the people be a bit more humble, not
so arrogant about their faith.
When you stand over a grave in that
cemetery, you look up and see this
building, where I sit now, where
people gather to sing of hope and
still bless God on hot afternoons
in August, on cold, snow covered days
in February, before carrying another
grandparent or husband or child out
across the road to that place of stones
and memories. This building too is a
sign. The living are not abandoned in
their grief. We come back here after
the journey, come back to hot dishes,
sandwiches, egg coffee, and pie.
Laughter can be heard.

Finally Fed

like hungry
little puppies
gobbling up
all we can
licking the dish
until it's dry
when we are
finally fed
the gospel

Roy Rogers

As long was Roy was around,
I was still a kid.
I always wanted to thank him.
But Roy died.
I don't get to thank him.
I don't get to be a kid anymore.

And the pastor said, before we go our separate ways,
let us stand and sing together...

A Convenant

A covenant, dear Church, a glorious promise.
By water, word God births you as God's own.
Now sing Christ's song, God's children of the promise;
Sing bold so God need never voice the stone.
Come, gather with God's many sons and daughters,
To hear Christ's word and share the food of God.
With friends to weep and friends to join in laughter.
Faith anchored deep within the cross's sod.

A covenant from God, a glorious promise.
Hope for our world, peace from God's very own.
Forgiveness from the Rabbi of the promise;
Grace gentle love to break our hearts of stone.
Tell people faith to laugh God's holy laughter,
Watch for the child and listen to the poor.
Kneel down before God's wounded sons and daughters.
With out-stretched arms, Christ's Church an open door.

A covenant, dear Lord, a glorious promise.
By water, word you claim us as your own.
Freed now to serve all people by the promise;
From death's fierce tomb you took away the stone.
You raised Christ up, and we will join in laughter.
Love has burst forth once buried in the sod.
Marked with Christ's cross as sons and as daughters,
We sing Christ's song held in the promise of God.

Text: Written by Gary A. Westgard
Tune: Londonderry Air
Music: Irish tune, arr. John Barnard, b. 1948

An Appreciation

I have wanted to put down in print, for some time, my appreciation for the care I, and my family, knew in the places we lived and worked for 35 years of ministry as a pastor in the Church. So, here it is. Thank you members of . . .

Farmington Lutheran Church in Farmington, Minnesota (Internship 1968-69)

United Lutheran Church in Laurel, Nebraska (1969-73)

Gayville Lutheran Church in Gayville, South Dakota (1973-80)

Bergan Lutheran Church at Meckling, South Dakota (1973-80)

Trinity Lutheran Church in Vermillion, South Dakota (1980-94)

Grace Lutheran Church in Watertown, South Dakota (1995-2004)

Thanks to Joe Mierau and Jenn Walker at Pine Hill Press for their guidance and kindness.

- Gary A. Westgard

About the Author

Gary Westgard was born in Rugby, North Dakota in 1940. When he was ten years old, his family moved to Longview, Washington. After high school, he attended the Lutheran Bible Institute in Seattle and Waldolf College in Forest City, Iowa. He graduated from Pacific Lutheran University at Tacoma, Washington, with a degree in Literature.

After graduating from Luther Seminary in St. Paul, Minnesota, in 1969, Gary served as a pastor in the Evangelical Lutheran Church in America for 35 years, retiring in 2004.

He and his wife, Vivian, live in Watertown, South Dakota, have two grown children, Christin and Joshua, a daughter-in- law, Lilla, and two grandchildren, Benjamin and Samuel.